MW01711053

Quality is a

Talking

Frog

Taking the Mystery out of

Quality Assurance

ISBN # 978-0-9822327-0-5

ISBN 978-0-9822327-0-5

About the Authors

Yes, they are brothers. Dennis and Sol have been working together, off and on, for their entire lives. But most recently, they have joined forces at the DTI Training Consortium. For the last ten years they have worked together to deliver their message on Quality Assurance to industry and governments around the world. A true situation where the sum of the parts greatly exceeds their individual talents, their seminars have been heralded as informative and greatly entertaining.

Dennis Taboada:

A native of New York, Dennis holds degrees in Telecommunications and Quality Assurance. As a professional Quality Assurance Specialist he began his career as a Quality Assurance Representative for the United States Department of Defense, Defense Logistics Agency. He also became an active member of the American Society for Quality Control, ASQC, where he wrote and taught QA seminars for industry.

While with the Department of Defense he was responsible for assuring the Quality of Mechanical, Electronic, Textile, Chemical and Fuel products for the United States Military. He was promoted within a few years to Master Instructor of Quality Assurance for the Defense Logistics Agency, Defense Contract Management Agency.

During this time he became a senior lead instructor and named subject matter expert by the U.S. Department of Defense in Quality Assurance. He was assigned by the United States State Department to teach Quality

Assurance courses for the Nation of Israel's, Israeli Defense Force in Tel Aviv, Israel.

Dennis became a fellow in the American Society for Quality and was named to be on the International Committee for the development of the Engineering Drawing specification ANSI/ASME Y14.5 for Geometric Dimensioning and Tolerancing.

He also was certified by the Registration Accreditation Board, RAB, as Lead Auditor for ISO 9000 and later lead assessor for the ISO 9000:2000 International specification. He also served on the first board of the US National Quality Award known as the Malcolm Baldridge Award.

Dennis left the Government in 1999 to become the CEO of his own training company, DTI Training Consortium. As President of DTI he has taught over 3,000 QA Specialists for the Defense Contract Management Agency, taught NASA engineers and QA specialists after the Columbia Space Shuttle disaster, Quality Assurance Principles to over 200 doctors of the United States Veterans Administration and Auditors of the Communication firm EarthLink.

The Government of Canada has recently tapped the knowledge of the brothers to bring the basics of what a good QA system should look like to all the Civil Aviation Inspectors of Transport Canada.

Sol Taboada:

The perfect complement to his brother, Sol has also proven to be his foil. While they agree on all the basic principles of Quality Assurance, they have been known to differ on delivery. Seminars often become very lively as the brothers, well, act like brothers.

A hardcore NY native, Sol has enjoyed the journey they have taken, especially traveling together presenting the Transport Canada Quality Assurance courses to TC inspectors. Their unique substance and style has proven to be a combination that has scored them high praise. Sol brings a varied background including, a degree in mathematics from the S.U.N.Y @ Stony Brook with practical applications in the development of industry best Quality Assurance curriculums and applications. His triumphs include programs with the United Sates Department of Defense, The U.S. Veterans Administration and their culture changing assignment of QA evaluation and instruction with The National Aeronautics and Space Administration (NASA)

With all this background, Sol still feels that his involvement with the efforts of Transport Canada will prove to be the crowning jewel in his extensive resume'.

Table of Contents

Preface

From Sol

What a strange name for a book on the technical science of Quality Assurance. Well, Dennis and I chose this name for its simplicity and true meaning. Once you get past chapter one, you too will understand. For now though, let me continue to tell you why we wrote this book, in this style.

Organizations and companies all strive to meet their customer demands for various levels of quality. Many companies actually achieve what they hope for, although, often it is by accident. Consultants the world over have made a fortune advising businesses, large and small alike, that a Quality Assurance system is imperative for their success. This is true, but they then parade out a display of technical procedures, complex statistical analysis tools and mathematically mind-blowing sampling and other charts that virtually insure that the company is either, one, going to hire the consultant to implement this system or, two, not implement any system. More injustices have been done to companies, and invariably their customers, in the name of "state of the art" system implementation than any economic or competitive hardship could ever reap.

Well, through our experience and travels across the world we have come to the conclusion that QA is not a state of mind, but a state of heart. Every company or organization should, and can, institute a QA system, because it is imperative to their long term survival. However QA systems can vary in size and complexity, just as companies vary.

Our goal here is to introduce to the small business, and reacquaint the large business, with what a basic QA system requires to be effective. Why this QA system will make their product, whether it is a manufactured item or a service provided, more appealing to their customer.

Quality Assurance will make you better, will make you leaner and very importantly, will make you more money.

We have conducted hundreds of seminars on this very topic and now have tried to capture our unique style in this book. It is written by both of us, and if you ever got to meet us, in many places you can tell who is writing what. One student of ours once labeled us as "good cop, bad cop" in our style. Whatever your take, we both care about this topic passionately, and hopefully it will show in our writing.

Preface

From Dennis

What happened to quality? When we think of quality the first thing that comes to mind is some sort of product. For example the Rolls Royce Silver Shadow, the Mona Lisa portrait and other quality icons. There is another aspect to quality that is equally, or more important. That is service quality. When was the last time you where served by someone in a business and received what you felt was excellent quality of service. Usually that experience is a rarity and related to the personality and persona of the person serving you. Is it possible to ALWAYS receive good quality service from a company no matter what day it is, or who is serving you? One of the closest attempts to quantify quality service has been initiated by the Disney Company. The product of the Disney Company is reflected in their "theatre" of presentation. Disney sells a fantasy, a feeling, an environment, thus its quality system is based more on theatrical presentation. Can a high quality level of service be achieved for each and every customer every time they are served. The word I like to use is "Quality Repeatability."

In my years of experience in quality I have noted some basic requirements you need to implement, that will always yield a desired result. In this book I will share some of those with you in hopes that you will be able to take away some tools that can be applied to your special circumstances and improve your quality system. Whether you are a provider of a product or service, these tools and ideas can make a difference. I say that, not based solely on my opinion, but rather through years of experience. As a student of many quality gurus I learned what works and what doesn't. The goal is to provide to your customers the most consistent high level of quality possible. Why? Perhaps a little boy from the backwoods of my home state can tell us........

Chapter One

The Frog

Once upon a time there was a boy walking through the forest. As he walked he happened upon a small pond. Sitting on a rock near the shore of the pond sat a frog. The young man picked up the frog and looked at it eye to eye. All of a sudden the frog began to speak.

"Oh young man I am so glad that you came along. I am really not a frog but beautiful princess that was beset with a curse. If you where to just kiss me, I would turn back into a princess and we would live happily ever after."

With that the boy took the frog and put it in his pocket and continued on his journey through the forest. In his pocket, the frog began to yell and complain.

"Hey! What are you doing! Get me out of here!"

Soon the boy stopped and pulled the frog out of his pocket and looked at it again. The frog spoke, "What is the matter with you? Did you hear what I said? I am a beautiful princess and all you have to do is just kiss me and we will live happily ever after."

The young man paused and then said to the frog.

“I’d rather have a talking frog!”

Sol and I have been conducting workshops for many years. We work best together and have found our method of presentation to be acclaimed by all those who we teach. Being brothers we tend to argue and banter in front of the class. To our surprise students enjoy this battle. Even though mom has always liked him best, the differing points of view, our “arguments”, always generate discussion.

This unique presentation style has actually worked against us. Many of our customers do not want classes from our company unless Sol and I present them. The story of the frog has a profound message and Sol and I begin to relate the lessons of the story in a way that brings a seemingly complex principle down to a basic level.

What are the lessons learned from this story? What did the frog have to offer? The frog had a product that it saw was needed by someone. The frog's market research indicated that a young man is the prime customer for its product. The frog was sure the boy wanted a beautiful princess to spend the rest of his life with.

What was the boy looking for? Well, the story really reveals that the boy wasn't looking for anything in particular. He happened upon this frog and decided in his world a talking frog was much cooler than a princess. The frog had not done the proper research.

How does this equate to customer quality? Companies often think they know what the customers really want. Without proper market research data it is impossible to know what your customer wants.

How many times has an entrepreneur come up with an idea and said to him or herself,

"Yeah, people really need this. So many people will want to buy this, I'll be rich." Only to realize that only a few really thought the product was needed!

One of the essential foundational cornerstones in which to build a quality system is the knowledge of what the customer wants. Your entire organization must know what the customer wants, the common goal, to serve our customers to point of customer delight!

As we look at building a quality system you will realize that what the customer wants, "is the mortar that holds the bricks of the system together." The simple moral to the story is this:

"Quality is defined by the Customer!"

Chapter Two

The Sap and the Tree!

"What is the best way to structure the Quality Program?"

During our seminars many participants ask Sol and I this very poignant questions.

Where “do I start? I mean, this sounds like a very complex program to create and I have limited time and resources.”

This is a very good question and one that is simple to answer. Start at the top! You may ask what does sap and the tree have to do with Quality Assurance.

Let us examine the complex inner working of a tree. I believe we can draw a great lesson on how a complex system can be made simple.

First, a tree is formed from a seed, an acorn. It grows up and sprouts leaves and creates a root structure that absorbs water and nutrients that work their way up the stem to the leaves. These nutrients provide the ingredients necessary for the leaves to undergo photosynthesis. Photosynthesis is the chemical reaction that forms important hydrocarbons, sugar, that feed the rest of the tree.

Ok so the tree will not grow unless it can produce food. The leaves are essential at the top of the plant. Once the food is produced, the food is then sent back down the stem or trunk to feed the rest of the tree. The roots are essential in order to provide the materials necessary to make the food and the sun is needed to initiate the food making process. I know this discussion should be limited to an Arbor Day oral report but it does provide a picture of the structure of the documentation necessary to grow and Quality Assurance system.

The Top of the Tree!

The Quality Assurance Manual

The Structure of the QA system should begin with the QA manual. Now the QA manual is the head of the system. The QA manual should give the companies ***Policies***. These policies should address the requirements, regulations and the wants of the customer. The manual should NOT give DETAILS on how the program would be carried out! The manual is simply stating what's in the QA program.

The following is an example of an entry in a QA Manual.

1.0 Responsibilities

1.1 The QA program is under the management of an appropriate person. The QA manager is responsible for the program and answers directly to the Chief Executive Officer. NOTE: For details and qualifications of the QA Manager see appendix D.

You will notice that the entry does not give details as to the qualifications of the QA manager but merely states that he or she is responsible. The statement in the QA manual is the policy regarding the person responsible for QA. Now the appendix D will have the current QA managers resume or some other document that will evidence the qualification of the QA manager.

The following is another example of how the Quality Assurance Manual should address requirements.

4.0 Calibration

4.1 *The Quality Assurance department shall be responsible for the calibration program and the accuracy of measurements in the company. Details of the calibration program our found in calibration manual C-1.*

You will notice that the paragraph consists of a simple broad sweeping statement that addresses the policy regarding calibration. Now, the calibration program requirements for the company will be delineated in a separate document. In this example manual C-1 would now address all the requirements for a calibration program.

The QA manual acts as the reference document to all the other detailed procedures in the company.

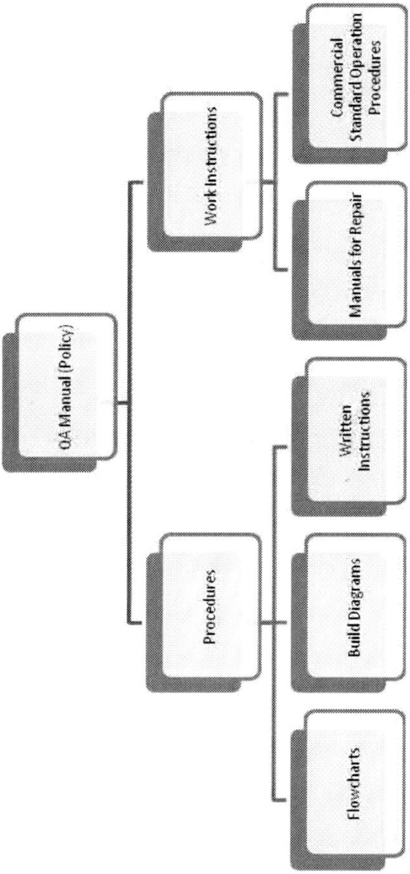

Example of a Quality Assurance Program Hierarchy

The QA manual is the starting point to find specific procedures on all of the departments in the company.

Let's take a look at the calibration example I just illustrated.

The QA manual simply states the calibration policy and intent. The QA manual then references the Calibration manual, C-1. The calibration manual will now delineate the specific requirements of the companies' calibration program. However, the calibration manual will NOT dictate how a SPECIFIC calibration will be performed. The calibration manual will reference the calibration procedures used for each instrument in the company.

Here is an example of the calibration manual reference.

C-1 2.0 Calibration Procedures

2.1 All calibration in the company will be done in accordance with the instruments usage manual. A list of all the measuring equipment used in the company is found in procedure C-2.2. In all procedures the instrument manuals will be out and utilized by the calibration technician.

You will notice that the calibration procedure references the instrument manual. This will now incorporate the instrument manuals into the entire QA system. You do not need to write procedures for calibration. The instrument manufactures' manual is the procedure. The intent of the QA system is to now incorporate those procedures into the Quality System. This is accomplished by a simple reference.

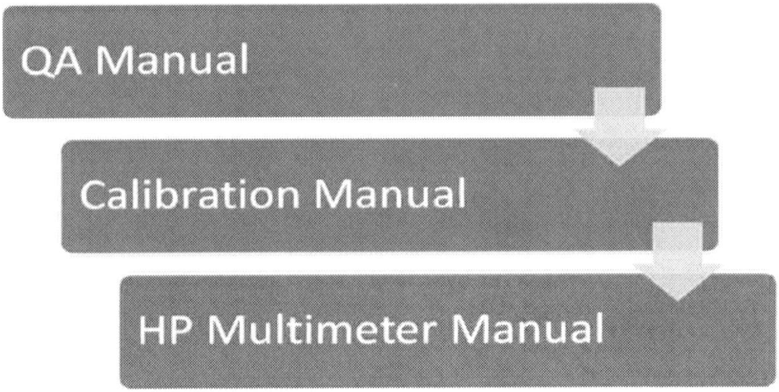

Keep in mind that the instrument manual could reference even a lower document. For example: the calibration of a multimeter will take into consideration environmental condition of the calibration. These environmental conditions would be found in the instrument's manual as well. Since the entire manual was reference in the QA system, all of the aspect and data in the manual is now incorporated into the Quality System.

BEWARE!

Incorporating a procedure into the Quality System now makes those procedure open game for auditing by the QA audit system and regulatory agencies.

So if you use a multimeter in your company, you must adhere to all the requirements of the multimeter's operational manual.

What should be in the Quality Assurance Manual?

This is a simple question to answer. The Quality Assurance Manual should address EVERY aspect of the customer's requirements. In the case of a regulated industry, the manual MUST address all the regulatory requirements of that industry that is applicable to the company. Now, remember that the QA manual just needs to address the requirements then lead us to the specific procedures that explain exactly how the requirements will be accomplished.

Another important item that needs to be in the QA manual is the specific standards required by the customer. The customer defines what standards the company must meet in order to purchase their product. Again these standards will be addressed in the QA manual and the specific HOWS will be addressed in the reference procedure found in the QA manual.

Finally we must address customer WANTS.

What is a customer want? In most industries customers communicate what they would want in a product or service. If a company is to maintain competiveness it must address customer wants. Let's face it. If a customer gets a want from company A, the chances of using company B diminish.

I can barely write my name!

How can I write a Quality Assurance Program?

Most companies have most of the procedures they need already written. These procedures are in the form of manufacturers' manuals, technical instructions, checklist and other documents. The key is put them in an organizational structure. The Quality Assurance manual need not be an expansive volume of verbiage. The Quality Assurance manual is simply the "card catalog" of the company's procedures.

I have friends, well maybe now former friends, which are consultants. Consultants help organizations meet regulatory requirements. Many consultants will offer to write your complete Quality Assurance System. They do this by using "Template Manuals" that are customized to your company. The problem with these template manuals is that they contain sections that are unnecessary for your operation. Also, be aware that what is placed into your manual now becomes law for you to follow. So, these well intentioned consultants may be doing you and your company a great disservice.

Step 1: Get your Regulations and Standards that are necessary for your company. Write down you customer desires and wants. All of the topics in your regulations and standards will be sections in your Quality Assurance Manual.

Step 2: Build only the sections of your manual. Use the regulation and standard headings to ***cross reference to your manual***. Also include a customer focused area to put the customer wants that are not covered in any regulation or standard. This cross reference is very important. Why? When the time comes for your regulatory agency to assess you, you want to make it as EASY as possible for them to find the regulations and standard requirements in your manual. The easier it is for the assessment team, the happier they will be.

You want your assessment team to be happy!!

Step 3: In each manual heading section begin writing the policy statements that correspond to the requirements in the regulation or standard.

Remember that the statements are policy and do not go into any detail as to how to do anything. Here is where you cite the reference to the procedures that will state how a task is done!

NOTE: You probably already have procedures that cover most of your regulatory and standard requirements. All you have to do is assign them document numbers that are easy to follow from the manual.

Step 4: Any areas that do not have procedures will require you to write them. Use flow charts, pictures or other easy means of communicating procedures. You may need to read the section in this book on creating procedures several times.

Let's walk through an example.

Let's say I wanted to see the procedure to replace the brakes on a Cessna 152. To find any specific procedure or work instruction you must be able to start at the Quality Assurance Manual. Follow the diagram below. The QA manual will have a section that gives the policy on repairing aircraft. The policy references a procedure that lists the repair manuals. Then the repair manual will have the procedure to replace the brakes. All procedures and instructions in the company should flow down from the QA manual in this manner.

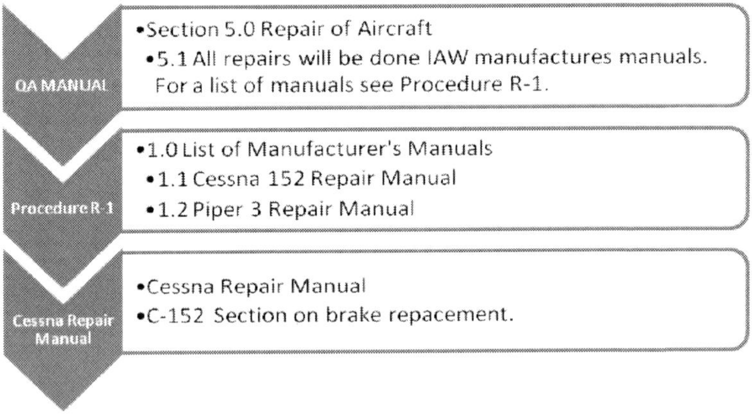

Conclusion

Creation of a documented Quality Assurance Program is not as hard as you think. I am willing to bet that you already have 70-90% of what is needed. Organization is the key. Remember the top of the tree is the Quality Manual. The Quality Manual sets the *policy* for the Quality Assurance Program.

To complete the analogy, the QA manual provides the food for the system to work. Those policies should *flow down* to the individual procedures, work instruction...etc. Those procedures and work instructions will state the how to do the work. It is important to realize that most of the procedures to perform work function are probably already written somewhere. They could be in manuals, specifications, books or even in your own files.

As the tree is living, so should your QA system be living. As you change procedures you must update the links between the procedures and the QA manual.

Procedures should always be checked to see if they are working. Remember, you have easy tools that you can use to determine if processes are in control and then tools to help improve the processes.

Don’t go out on a limb by hiring consultants that will write your manuals for you. It can be very expensive in a number of ways. Nobody knows what your company does better than you. Be firmly rooted in the profound knowledge of your companies systems by writing the system yourself. There are tools to help you accomplish this task. These tools are in this book.

Chapter 3

The Lessons of the "F's"

*A*s we go about the world explaining our concepts regarding QA, Dennis and I are confronted often with the challenge of demonstrating what a good system does, and, is it worth the money? Many of our audience members are from small organizations and regard the implementation of an effective QA system as an expense. They have been exposed to consultants and lecturers who speak of confusing statistical analysis and high brow mathematics. It is a shame, as most of these proponents are afraid to tell the general public that effective QA is really a simple task.

While we can explain for hours how simple it is and what the benefits can be if properly installed, but, we have found an excellent exercise that demonstrates a great many of these principles, and is so simple that everyone feels like it is some thing they can do.

The majority of the text that will follow is how we conduct the "F" exercise live during a class. I decided to write it mostly as a script with explanations. I think you will find it interesting and entertaining.

Setting the Scene

In our seminars, we try to schedule this exercise right after our first lunch break. As the participants come back, we usually start by telling a little story about ourselves. Usually its something a little humorous, and then I segue into this....

"During the break, Dennis and I were discussing the composition of this class. We were very impressed by the experience and qualifications of the participants. Typically in our workshops a portion of the group are required to be here to complete some certification or other. Another few are here just to get out of work for a couple of days, but I think that most of you are here because you really want to understand what QA is. To me that makes you very caring people, probably some of the best in your industry. I will take it even a step further; I told Dennis

that I think this group is possibly, "the best of the best".

Since this group is so exceptional, let me ask you a question. If you owned a company and had a very important customer order 10 of a particular item your company produces, how would you assure that he was completely satisfied with his purchase? How would you make sure that he received 10 of the exact item he ordered, free from defects? How would you make sure he was happy?"

Typically, discussion begins about inspecting the products in one way or another, with an eventual consensus that since this customer is very important, and it is only ten items, one hundred percent inspection would be the best approach. In other words, we would take the time to look at each and every piece thus insuring good product.

"Well since I am the CEO of this company and a very busy man, I really don't have the time to look at these

items myself. I think I might have to hire professional inspectors to do the looking for me. I would look for the best inspectors, the best people I could find to look at them. I might even hire "the best of the best".

I am going to pass out a simple procedure, one that I wrote. I want you to read and perform the instructions on this procedure. Your job is to do this procedure as rapidly as possible, discuss your results with no one. Don't let your co-worker influence your findings. When everyone is done, I will ask you for your results. Since I hired the best of the best, I am confident that our results will reflect the quality of our personnel."

At this point we pass out the procedure below and wait for the class to complete it. Should a discussion arise about clarification on the procedure, we shut it down, telling them to just do the procedure. Sometimes we use humor to direct them to accomplish this simple procedure.

Why don't you try the procedure on the next page yourself, before you continue reading, it will make the discussion that follows more relevant.

100% *Inspection Techniques*
Is it the Best Inspection Technique?

Inspection Exercise

Instructions: In the following paragraph , simply count the number of "F's" that appear. Write your results at the end of the paragraph in the space provided.

"Foremost of the First Forefathers Faltered in and of their Faith in the foundation of the Federation. The First Forefathers Failure of Faith was of Finding Fault with the infancy of the Foundations and of the Freedoms formed by the Federation. Often these First Fault was so Followed by Failure to define the Foremost of the Fundamental infractions of Faith, that often are infringements of Freedom to fellow officers of the Federation. Often Futile refinement of Freedoms end up infringing on Fundamental foundations of Faith defined in and of the Federation's Founders. Most of all we must not Fail in refining the First Fundamental Foundations of our Faith, If we fail we shall definitely Falter in Finding the Faith of Freedom!"

Please write the number of "F's" you found here: ________

During the time the class is working on the count, I write all their names on a white board or easel at the front of the room and prepare to collect their data. Once they are all done we begin the process.

"All right guys, I am ready for the results. Having the best of the best here gives me a great confidence in my results. OK, Bill let's start off with you…what did you get!

Bill = 78 ***Great Bill,***

now you Joe…

Joe = 39

39? Joe did I give you the same procedure? 39?

Sam what did you get?

Sam = 0

Zero!!!, holy cow, what's going on here.

Continue collecting numbers from the class members making comments about the vast differences of their answers and when you're done, there is typically a result like I have listed below.

Bill = 78	Joe = 39
Sam = 0	Judy = 78
Jose = 77	Derek = 39
Mildred = 78	Mike = 0
Evan = 78	Gary = 0
Lisa = 77	Bob = 39
Frank = 78	Sue = 0
Pete = 78	Carol = 39

Once I've collected all the results, I typically stand back and look at the variation and shake my head wondering what is going on with the results. I then decide I need a better view of these results and plot the production points on a graph in order to get a clearer look. This chart should like this.

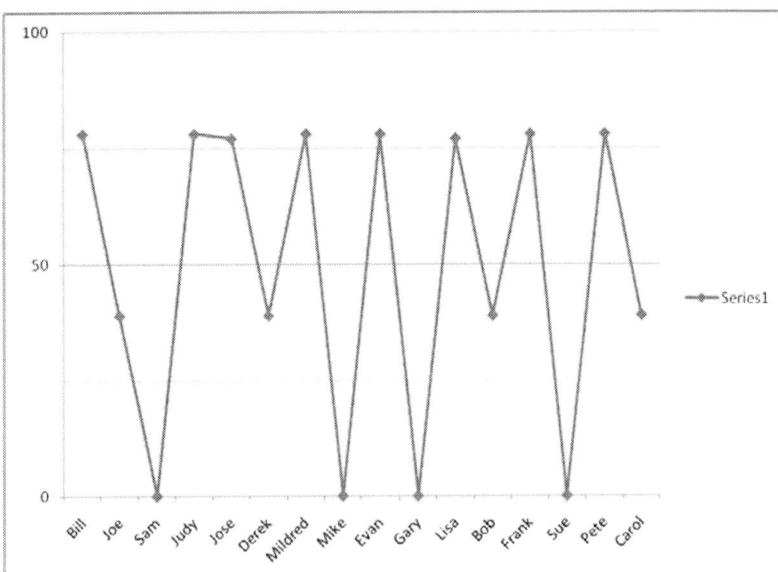

The graph on the previous page, known as a Run Chart, now shows with exclamation, the variation of our class results. The dialogue I use continues below.

"Holy Cow! Look at this variation. What do you think about this? Does this result show a procedure that is in control? Is our result in Control?"

There is usually a lot discussion, laughter and people trying to explain why this result looks the way it does. The overall consensus, and I've done this exercise hundreds of times, is that we are totally out of control.

"Let me ask you this, if I fired all of you and brought 16 new inspectors in, how would the output look? What if I brought in 100 more inspectors, what would the output look like then?

The answer coming from the participants states that the results would be the same no matter how many different people I brought in.

"So, I ask you again. Is this procedure in control?

The answer is yes, the result shown here based upon this procedure are in complete control!

No matter how many inspectors I brought in the output would look the same. We would have a variation that would extend somewhere between 0 and 80 or so. Armed with this information if I had to sell my F's I could price them.

These results are dependable, however they are not acceptable.

Let's do some math. If it costs $1.00 to produce each of your outputs the total cost for this production run would be $16 (16 students x's $1.00).

Now, if we could only sell results that equal 78 we would have a saleable output of 6 from the results given by Bill, Judy, Mildred, Evan, Frank and Pete.

That means the cost to produce a saleable output would be $2.67 per unit of 78 ($16 for the run / 6 saleable units).

In order to make a decent profit we would have to sell the units for $8.01 ($2.67 x 3).

But let's look at this chart and see the variation.

I see we have a number of you who found zero F's. Sam, I see you got zero, how did you arrive at that answer?"

The typical answer to this question is that he was looking for "F's" in the paragraph, that is the quote marks and everything in between or he was looking for F's including the apostrophe.

Now I turn on a apologetic tone and explain...

"I'm sorry, I was not looking for that, I was looking for F's, plural. Perhaps I didn't explain myself properly.

Now that you know that what do you think your result might be?"

The answer is usually 77 or 78. The new Run Chart would look like this, moving all the zero's to 78.

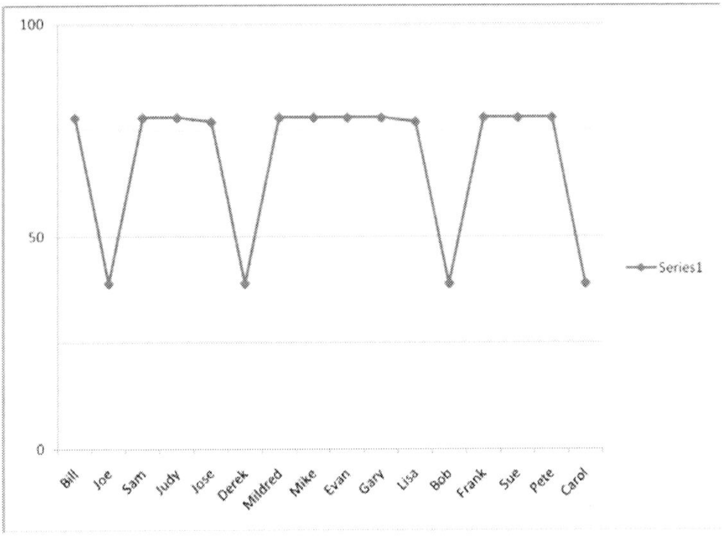

"Now, let's look at the people who got 39. Bob, I see that you got 39, how did you arrive at that number?"

The typical answer for this number is that the inspector was looking for capital F's.

"Oh! I'm sorry, I was looking for F's, all f's, capital and lower case. I guess I didn't explain myself well enough.

Now that you know this what do you think your answer might be?"

The response is usually again 77 or 78.

Based upon this new clarification the 39's move to 78 and our run chart looks like this.

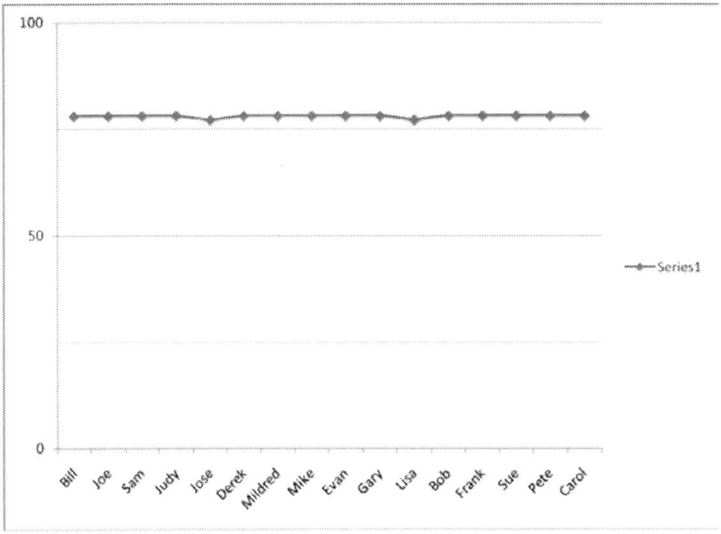

Now that we have this new defined run, let's look at the economics of this shrinking of the variation.

We now have 14 saleable F's at a new net cost of $1.14 to produce (16 units / 14 saleable).

With this new cost we can now sell our product for $3.43 ($1.14 x's 3) and be more competative in the marketplace or if the market will bear the original sale price of $8.01 our profit increase is incredable. And all this was accomplished with little or no capital expense to our company. We just produced a pictoral representation of our process from production data we are compiling anyway, and examined it.

Noticing the extreme variation we took analysis action to see why it was so significant. Finding out that our procedure was too vague we tightened the controls and achieved startling results.

Will we ever be able to achieve no variation?

No, there will always be someone miscounting or otherwise skewing the data line.

However, any company can achieve similar results by using these tools. It is just another way of looking at our output and deciding if there is room for improvement. The original result of our F experiment looked to be completely out of control, but we discovered that actually it was a very NORMAL result. All written procedures produce normal variation, the question is, is that variation acceptable?

Getting a little deeper into the analysis, once we stabalized our output, like we did after our analysis, we could begin using more sophisticated monitoring tools like Control Charts.

These charts calculate the statistical upper and lower control limits on a process output and help identify problems and point out trends.

Here is a an example of a chart on the last production run, where we had adjusted our 0's and 39's to 78. Note the calculated Upper and Lower Control limits the median line and the units selected to be out of control.

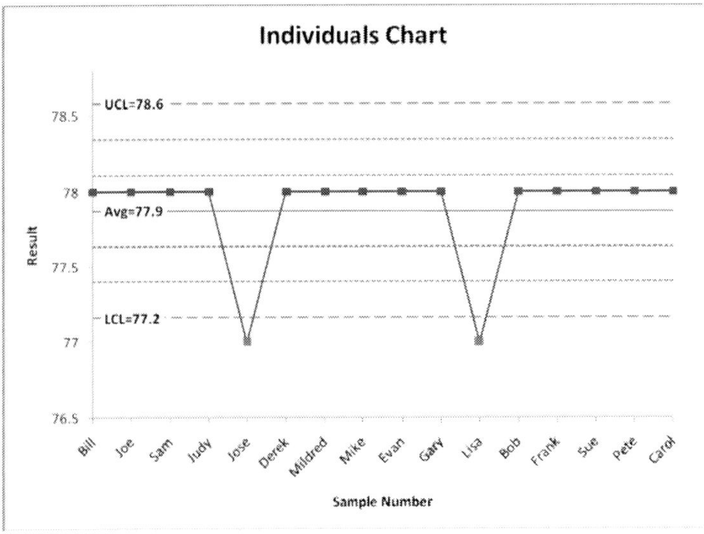

What are lessons we learn from the “F” exercise? Here they are:

#1. A documented procedure, when followed properly, ALWAYS produces a “NORMAL” outcome.

When we mention normal, what we mean is that the result of the process is PREDICTABLE!

The result is not necessarily good, but it is predictable. Our prediction may show that our output will be bad, but the bottom line is we will know! We will talk about this predictability more in a later section.

#2. When we have a normal system the system is said to be “IN CONTROL.” In control means that we can predict the outcome and that we can affect the system by changing the procedure either for good or bad. As we saw in the results of the exercise, the variation was great due to the fact that some interpreted the instructions differently. When we clarified, or changed, the instructions what happened to the variation? Yes, the variation was reduced. Now we not only predict the outcome but the variation of our prediction is reduced so now we have much better control of the process and know almost the exact result we desire. Remember we can never totally reduce variation due to human factors.

#3. 100% inspection only yields about 95 percent quality outcome. It is important to know that looking at everything that is done does not assure everything will be good. Variation will always occur. By knowing this fact we can reduce oversight and still yield a good confidence level of the quality of our process.

“Knowledge is Power”

Francis Beacon

Quality begins with knowledge. Knowledge of your system, your process and personnel. Dr. Edwards W. Deming say, “Without *Profound Knowledge* of a process, any changes are simply *Tampering*.”

Chapter 4

Of Rockets and

Hamburgers

"An Experiment in Developing the Best Procedures"

Whether it is baking a cake, building a hamburger, or building a rocket, you need clear and concise procedures.

Clear procedures are essential to producing a product that meets your standards and ultimately the customer's needs and wants. Keep in mind that the product could be a service you provide.

As we have already learned, documented procedures assure that your customer requirements are met *consistently.* They also provide the means to predict the outcome of a process.

In our seminars Sol and I talk about the importance of documented procedures to communicate to the workers just how a task or process is to be done. I ask the students, "Have you ever been to McDonalds?" Of course most answer yes! The next time you go into a McDonalds or any other successful fast food restaurant by the way, look beyond the front counter to the back. That is where food construction is in full production. You will see very colorful laminated cards taped to the walls. If you look carefully you will see these cards have pictures of hamburgers, tacos and other foods depending on what the restaurant makes. These cards show the food in various stages of production.

These cards provide two essential elements in producing a consistent product.

First, they provide a standard. They show the willing workers what the finished product should look like. There is nothing better for the level of employee to follow than a high resolution picture of a Big Mac®.

Second they provide the step-by-step procedure to assure that the products are made the *same way every time*. Some restaurants use "exploded views" to show the proper sequence of components. I particularly like exploded views. I feel they convey an abundance of information.

Who said the following?

"Procedures, when followed, always produce a normal output."

That's right, I did!

The preparation procedures you will find in fast food establishments are generally in pictorial form. They are primarily this way because it is the easiest way to communicate to the willing workers exactly how to build the product, and what the finished product should look like.

This started me thinking of the best ways to communicate a procedure to the workforce entrusted to follow them.

My thoughts led me to the title of this chapter, "How to build a rocket."

Sol and I were asked to teach a seminar by NASA at Kennedy Space Center. In this seminar I wanted to illustrate the best method of communicating a procedure in the production of a product. One night I stopped by a local toy store and picked up a set of children's building blocks. I knew this would work for my students because they were designed for 2 year olds and up (oops, just made a few more enemies). During this time in Florida, Sol had brought his family, including his 17 year old step daughter and her friend to soak up a little sun. I brought the blocks to them and asked them to build a rocket. They did! I then reversed engineered the rocket and wrote a very detailed procedure on the construction of the rocket.

(Side note: It is important that written procedure use words and terminology that can easily be understood by the reader. This reminds me of the story of a group of monks who met one night for dinner at the monastery. The head monk asked the others, "Where is Brother Peter?" another monk replied, "he is in the basement studying the scrolls." The head monk requested, "Please get Brother Peter and till him it is time to sup." As the brother entered the basement, there was brother Peter crying over the scrolls scattered before him. The monk responded, "Brother Peter what is the matter? Why are you so upset?" Brother Peter tearfully replied, "The word is CELEBRATE!!")

OK back to the procedure.

After I completed the written procedure, I made a performance specification. The performance specification gives a detail description of the product and in most cases how the product is to perform. In our experiment the rocket performance specification was limited to the appearance. Obviously if I had a performance specification for its function that would be a lot more complex and take more time then allowed by the seminar.

Finally, I simply took several pictures of the completed rocket from different angles. I gave the instruction to the team, “Build this.”

The very next day we divided the class into three groups. I gave a set of building blocks to each group.

The first group had the blocks with just the written detailed procedure on how to build the rocket.

The second group had the blocks with just the performance specification to guide them to build the rocket.

The third group had the picture of the rocket with the instructions "build this."

Here were the results of the experiment.

TEAM 1: The team with the written procedure took the longest to accomplish the build of the rocket. They were very close to the actual product we had intended for them to build. They had some minor errors that were due to misinterpretation of the procedure, much like the word "celebrate." This group also did not have any collapses of the block structure, because the procedure had the proper order to make the build balance properly while under construction. This is an important revelation. The written procedure can actually direct the sequence of the build which may be essential in the case of specific techniques necessary to make the build easier. Another lesson that was revealed from this team was the errors made. We had talked about interpretation of procedures causing variation. Results of ambiguities in this procedure caused the same errors to occur every time I conducted the experiment. Remember even with the errors in build, the output is still “normal” and *predictable*. If I do not change the procedure, the errors in building the rocket will always be there.

TEAM 2: This team had the performance specification. The resulting rocket was the furthest away from the desired finished product, but met the requirements of the performance specification. I noticed that this team did have some trouble in the construction of the rocket. They occasionally would drop some of the blocks while stacking. It was more of a trial and error process. This team was the second to finish the rocket.

TEAM 3: This is the team that had only the photographs of the finished product. They finished the fastest but, they also had a problem with dropping the blocks during stacking.

Why did team 2 and 3 have a problem with dropped blocks and team 1 did not?

It turns out that in the actual written procedure I put special instruction to carefully place two blocks simultaneously to keep the stack balanced. Team 2 did not have these instructions since they were working to the performance specification. Team 3 just had the photographs so they did not know of the balance problem in the stacking of the blocks.

What are the lessons learned from this simple exercise?

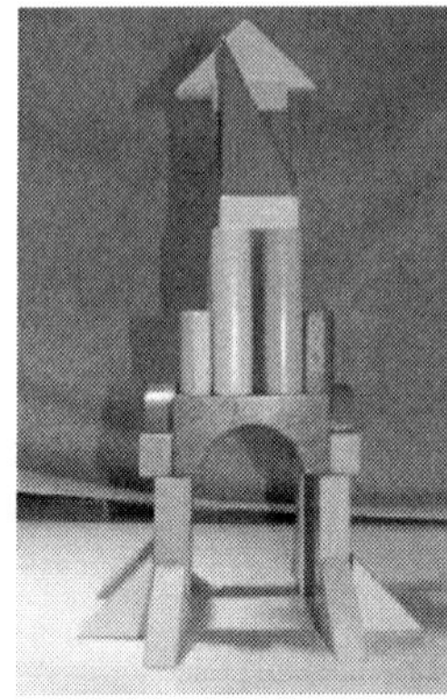

First, written procedures provide the best detail information in performing a task but take a long time to read and interpret. The written procedure, if not written clearly or precisely can lead to error.

I should note here that even a poorly written procedure, when followed, will produce a "normal" output as we previously have seen.

The performance specification gives a lot of freedom to the method and configuration the user can use to achieve the performance requirements. It also can backfire if a desired characteristic is omitted from the specification. The photographs provided the best result for conveying the desired finished product; however it did not convey essential building techniques necessary to assure the smooth assembly of the finished product therefore causing production problems, the dropped blocks.

So what do we learn from this little experiment? The application is simply this. Procedures can be a *combination* of written instruction in conjunction with pictures and performance characteristics. The entire goal of the procedure is to produce a "predictable" output. If we can design a procedure using combinations of tools, we can greatly narrow the variation of the output significantly.

Stock Photo

This experiment not only provides excellent guidance to procedure writing, but also to *creating* them which is far more artistic. By applying the principles of documented communication we can design procedures not only to build things but also to fill out documents, assign workloads, ship items...etc. The documented procedure guidance can be applied to all process applications.

The question has been asked, "How detailed should these procedures be? I mean aren't we "*dumbing*" down the system?" The answer is very simple. If you were to fire everyone in your company, the new crew should be able to use the procedures to produce the same output or product. Yes, the resulting production will be slower but the product should be the same.

<u>The key is to make the procedure so that its intended audience can understand it.</u>

Have you ever purchased a product that required assembly? If so, then you will fully understand the importance of clear and concise assembly procedures.

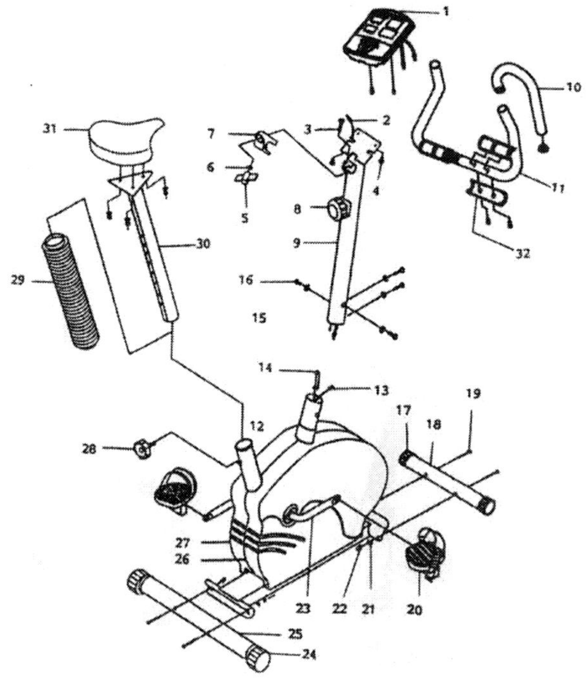

Exploded view of exercise bike provided by stock images.

The most common method for communicating build requirements is the use of the exploded view. Though the exploded view shows the configuration of all parts and how they fit together, this view does not show how the parts fit together. This is where the written portion of the procedure is essential. The written procedure will fill in the blanks left by the picture.

So what is the bottom line? Procedures are essential to assure normal predictable outputs. These procedures must be in a form that everyone can follow. They should be clear and to the point. These procedures need to be reviewed to assure they are achieving the desired outcome. Think outside the box in the design of these procedures.

And referring back to the statement, “how far do I have to dumb down this procedure?”. Well, if your goal is to make consistently good product or output, then wouldn’t it be SMART to make the procedure understandable to the expertise of the employee doing it!

Chapter 5

Through the Looking Glass

"Turning your procedures into

Audit Checklists"

OK, you have all the procedures written. How do I audit them? This is where the audit checklist comes in. Remember that the quality system must have a way of being audited. That is why we have procedures for all processes in the company.

Those procedures now need to be transformed into checklists that will be used to audit the procedure. In this section I hope to give you the tools necessary to transform those procedures into audit checklists.

I must begin this section by first expressing my opinion on audit checklist writing. It is my belief that the audit checklist is best written by the department that is actually doing the procedure. This is a controversial belief. The staunch quality assurance philosophy is that the audit checklist must be written by the quality assurance department in order to be totally independent.

I disagree and I have my reasons.

First: In keeping with the philosophies of the great quality gurus like Dr. Deming who say,

"Nobody knows a process better than the person or persons doing the process." The people responsible for following a particular procedure are the ones who best know that procedure. With a little help in audit checklist writing, those people can invariable make the best checklists.

Second: If the department that is responsible for the procedure writes the checklist, how can there be any argument as to the validity of a finding against that checklist. Yes this will alleviate problems with future audit findings.

Third: By having the individual departments write the audit checklist, the quality assurance system will be developed much faster. Keep in mind that this is the least significant reason.

Now let's take a look at the nuts and bolts of transforming a procedure into an audit checklist.

The key to writing audit checklists is to determine what the end product of the procedure should look like, first. I have received a lot of calls from small companies that are trying to implement a self audit system. It doesn't matter how small or big your company is, the audit checklist producing process is the same. I will illustrate several examples of audit checklists.

The first is for the small company. Companies we commonly call "mom and pop" shops.

To apply for a leave of absence:

Requester	**1**	Complete a *Leave of Absence* form.
	2	Submit the form to your section supervisor.
Supervisor	**3**	Review the *Leave of Absence* form and add your recommendation in the box provided at the bottom of the form, if appropriate.
	4	Forward the form to the District Manager for authorization.
Manager	**5**	Review the form and authorize the leave, if appropriate, by signing the bottom of the form.
	6	Return the form to the section supervisor.
Supervisor	**7**	Notify the requester of the decision.
	8	If the leave was granted, notify the Payroll Department of the leave, including the expected date of return, and the requester's pay status.

Here is a very simple procedure for employees to request a leave of absence. This is a good example procedure for us to create a very simple audit checklist. Simply follow the procedure and ask yourself if each step has been performed or not. The audit checklist simply adds the questions.

To apply for Leave of Absence:

		YES	*NO*
Requester	1. Complete a *Leave of absence* from.	☐	☐
	2. Submit the form to your section supervisor.	☐	☐
Supervisor	3. Review the *Leave of absence* form and add your recommendations in the box provided at the bottom of the form, if appropriate.	☐	☐
	4. Forward the form to the district manager for authorization.	☐	☐
Manager	5. Review the form and authorize the leave, if appropriate, by signing the bottom of the form.	☐	☐
	6. Return the form to the supervisor.	☐	☐
Supervisor	7. Notify the requester of the decision.	☐	☐
	8. If the leave was granted, notify the payroll department of the leave. Including the expected date of return, and requester's pay status.	☐	☐
		Comments	

LOOK HOW SIMPLE!

This was a very basic example of a checklist created against the previous procedure. Most would say that this is a "cop out." But, is it really?

If the Quality Assurance audit function simply verifies that the procedure is being followed, isn't that the goal of the audit. The audit is assuring that the procedure is followed.

It is important to realize that creating this checklist was not a very hard to do. We must keep in mind that not all procedures will lend themselves to easy checklist writing. Some procedures will require a more complex check and balance system.

The following is another example of a real procedure that will need to be audited.

2.3 Baggage Handling Procedure.

"Aircraft loading will be estimated by the baggage count formula for each compartment and recorded on the baggage weight distribution record for that flight."

The audit checklist must verify this statement. There are several ways to accomplish this. First, the auditor could simply pull a sample of the weight distribution records for a given aircraft or period of time and check the record to see if the loaders recorded the proper data.

Second the audit could also be performed concurrent to the actual operation. In this case the checklist can simply be an observation record of the procedure.

Here is an example of an audit checklist for this procedure line.

2.3 Baggage Handling Procedure Audit Checklist.

1. Pull a statistical sample of weight distribution records and observe records of weights based on the baggage count formula for each compartment .Are all the records filled out correctly? YES NO COMMENT

2. (If concurrent). Does the baggage count formula reflect the actual baggage count in each compartment? YES NO COMMENT

3. Is the baggage weight distribution record accurate according to the baggage count formula? YES NO COMMENT

Remember that the actual baggage handling and loading personnel are the best qualified to help write the checklist.

What if the procedure is in flowchart form? In the case of flowcharts, we must focus in on the process flow and decision process of the procedure. Here is an example of a flowchart procedure:

5.1 Incoming phone call procedure.

Figure 1:
Part of an example flow chart showing how to route incoming phone calls

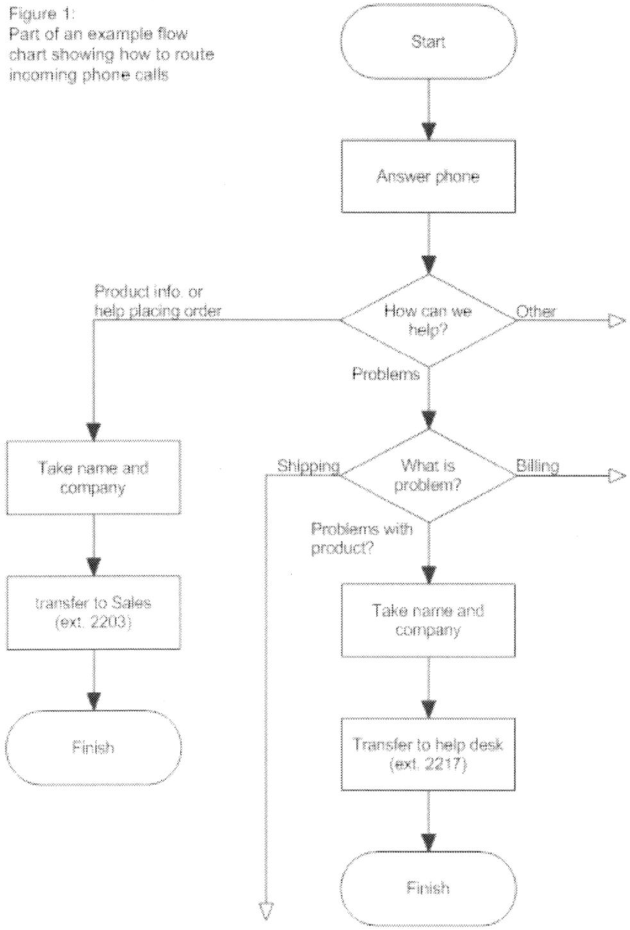

Writing the audit checklist to a flow chart is a little more difficult, but not unachievable.

In order to make the assessment of a flowchart we must first discuss the concept of "OBJECTIVE EVIDENCE."

Objective Evidence

Is a particular process critical and what I mean by critical is this, the process, if NOT accomplished or accomplished correctly, will inevitably lead to bigger problems down the line? If so, then we need to inject an audit point here. In my seminars I use the example of the cleaning process before painting. If the cleaning process is not accomplished correctly the paint will not adhere causing more time consuming and costly repair and rework. So the cleaning process must have some "Objective Evidence" that it has been accomplished correctly.

This evidence can be accomplished in two ways. First, an inspection point can be added to the process to make sure the cleaning was done correctly.

Second, a "LOG" or entry data point is established to record specific readings or just documentation of the process.

This record is auditable by the QA department and more important serves as objective evidence that the critical operation was accomplished.

These records should be acted upon by management. For example, if the log is not filled out management should find out why and correct the cause. If the logs are "penciled whipped" then don't even bother keeping them.

These logs may seem to be tedious to fill out but, they will prove to be a source of consistency and discipline which will improve the predictability of your product and/or service. Here we have an example of a simple log you all have seen before.

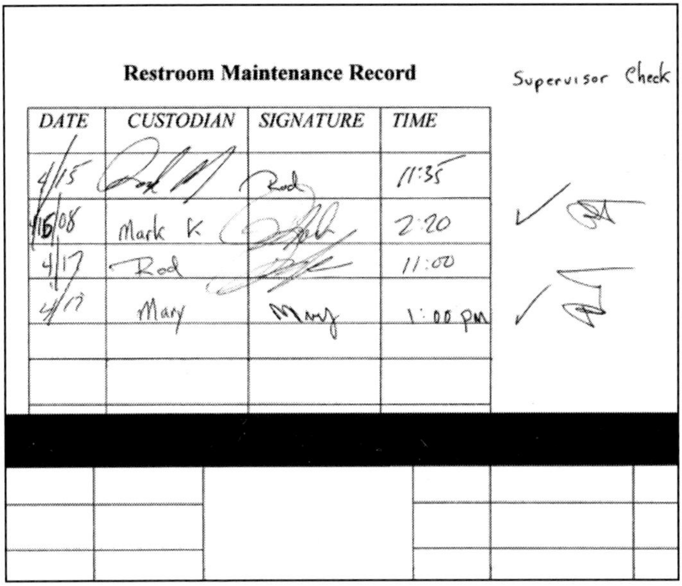

Restroom Maintenance Record

Supervisor Check

DATE	CUSTODIAN	SIGNATURE	TIME
4/15	[illegible]	Rod	11:35
4/16/08	Mark K	[illegible]	2:20
4/17	Rod	[illegible]	11:00
4/17	Mary	Mary	1:00 pm

[redacted]

It is obviously important to this company to have its restrooms maintained. So the addition of a simple log serves several purposes:

1. The log motivates the maintenance staff to perform the operation.

2. The log serves as “Objective evidence” that the operation was complete

2. The Supervisor check provides an additional incentive to perform the operation

and to make sure that it is performed to management standards.

4. The maintenance technician is now an "Owner" of the process.

5. If the operation was not completed, the record will serve to help find the root cause of the failure.

I know what you're thinking. This is a very simple and low priority process. Yes, but think of the benefits the simple log will reap in your "critical processes."

All logs will become part of your permanent records. It is important to review them during your audits in order to catch trends that might occur.

The following log has been provided by a power company regarding a diesel generator.

__________Power Company
Generator 15A Daily Oil Check

Date	Technician		Oil Level	TIME	Signature
9/27/07	Brian James	9/10	90%	7:58 AM	
10/1/07	Brian James	7/10	70%	9:00 AM	
10/4/07	Tommy Figure	6/10	60%	7:59	
10/6/07	Brian Jame	5/10	50%	8:35	
10/8/07	Christina Brown	4/10	40%	8 AM	
10/10/07	Tommy Figure	3/10	35%	7:41	
NO	RECORD NEEDED		ENGINE	SEIZED	!

" Logs and Records un-checked, can lead to results that wreck" *Author unknown*

Don't just store the records. The QA program should review records periodically to help improve the system. Continuous improvement of the system is essential to more efficiency and cost savings.

The flowchart example of the incoming phone calls should be audited by inserting logs after critical processes and check to see if the decisions made were per the procedure.

Here is an example of the checklist for the flowchart a few pages back as it would be audited concurrent:

Procedure 5.1 Audit checklist

1. Are calls being routed properly per procedure? *Yes* ☐ *No* ☐

2. Is the company information recorded for sales calls? *Yes* ☐ *No* ☐

3. Are problem call being routed properly? *Yes* ☐ *No* ☐

4. Is the company information recorded for problem calls *Yes* ☐ *No* ☐

This audit checklist is generic. Keep in mind that your checklists will be designed to meet the goals of the department under audit and ultimately the company. By following the procedures that were designed for the specific process, you assure that the output of that department is predictable and consistent.

The introduction of logs will provide the necessary objective evidence of process consistency. Ultimately your company will become more efficient and out-of-control trends will be stopped before they become disasters.

Chapter 6

Taking a Picture

We've talked about analyzing data, shrinking variation and numerous other aspects of improving the system. All this is fine and dandy, but none of it can occur without something to analyze.

Every organization collects data, some of it from sales or costs, other as production results and some as administrative functions, just to name a few.

In a good QA system, data collection, let me restate that, *complete data collection,* is at the core to getting meaningful results.

As we stated earlier a procedure, and everything we do is a procedure, when quantitatively analyzed, will produce a normal output.

While most small businesses can tell when something is going good or bad, it is sometimes much better to get a picture, an EKG, so to speak, of the processes. The axiom that a picture is worth a thousand words is especially true in business.

As we observed doing the F exercise, problems with a procedure are so apparent when you can visualize them.

Before we can paint the picture we need to gather the data. We have found that most businesses today gather all kinds of information. Some use it a matter of course, others gather it to archive it for some future use. Whatever the case, we do have our first suggestion on how to prepare to use this information for our QA system.

Most computers no matter how inexpensive come with some kind of data management software. We recommend that you use fields to capture your data. For example employee names can be captured in fields listed as FirstName, MiddleName and LastName. Social Security Numbers can be captured in a field called SS# and so on. Measurements, test grades and any quantitative metrics can be captured this way, along with attribute data like Go/No Go data. The beauty of this is that it is easily recalled by any other program to use in analysis.

This system also allows for streamlining processes since acquisition of data need not be duplicated. All in all, a data capture system is the easiest way to start a good QA system because it makes everything that comes later, the analysis, the mystical statistical analysis, so much easier to achieve.

Let's take a look at exactly how we could accomplish this.

Let's say we hire a new employee. Typically the first thing he does is fill out a form with his personal information. If all this data is entered in fields, we can recall it later as needed after he has been worked into the system. Now, let's say his job is to perform some kind of shop manufacturing making widgets. (Actually, I hate the term widgets, so I think I'll call them do-dads). So the employee is making do-dads and every do-dad he makes will have serial number to identify the part and a code to identify the machinist who produced the part. Later on in the process measurements may be taken on these do-dads and these would be recorded using the serial number of the part to continue the "unbroken chain" of traceability.

Once again later on in the process we have multiple days of production with everything having been tracked throughout production. Management then can recall data on specific measurements, or specific dates or production runs easily by entering the field names he wants to analyze and using simple analysis programs to view trends anomalies that may become apparent. These products can then be traced to specific machines or machinists that may need repair or additional training.

So the bottom line here is that if we just take the time to organize ourselves so that data captured is placed in easily recallable fields, our analysis process just became much easier. If you don't really know all that is available in this field there are tons of books and courses that will explain the process. Computer programs that will organize and store this data are available in all sizes and costs. I have seen a company of 3 persons get a basic data program for less than $300. There is no need to go overboard at first.

So, this brick in the foundation of a good QA system is easy to set up.

Established companies may have a little more work getting past data into the system, but they will soon see why it is imperative they do.

Newer companies will have an easier time, but no matter what, the path to a more efficient company will have been cleared.

Now that we have all this data gathered and stored let's spend some time looking at all the possible analysis tools, snapshots to coin a phrase, that we can use to better visualize our processes.

The Pareto Chart

We're going to use the same data gathered from the F exercise of Chapter 3 to produce the chart below.

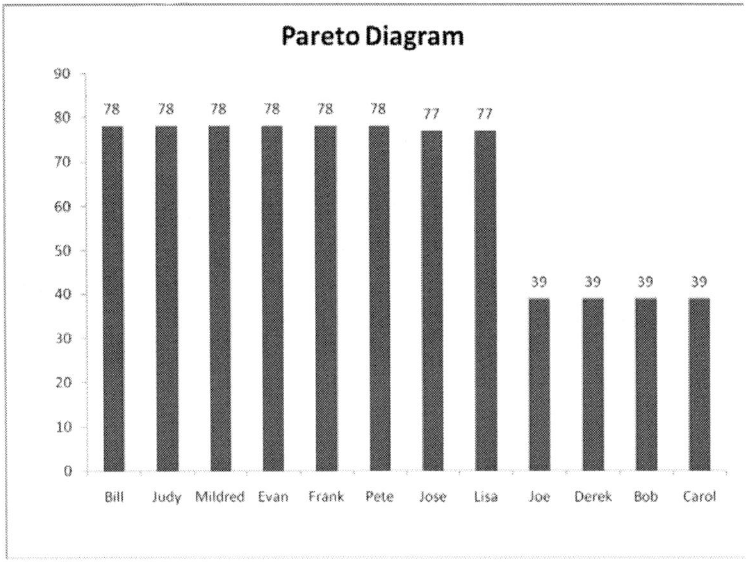

Notice how the chart has moved like amounts together. This brings to the forefront the variation among the results. Looking at it we can quickly see that are indeed groupings of results that are similar, in fact we are missing 4 results as they were not displayed because of the zero result they attained.

What this helps us to see are which results we need to pay attention to, or as they saying goes, “it separates the vital few from the trivial many”.

It is obvious from this graphic that we must address those four workers who got 0 as their result first. Then the four who got 39 would be the next objective. Because, if you remember 78 was the desired result.

Histogram

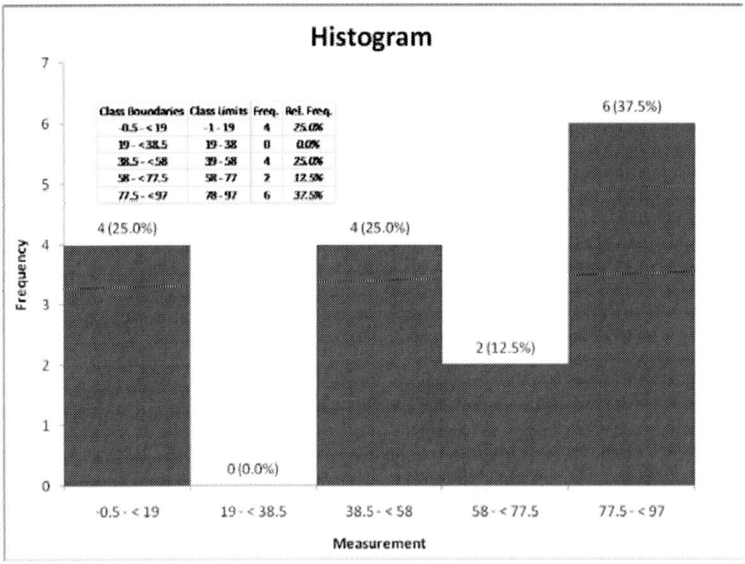

Here we have a simple graphic, known as a histogram. I used to think that a histogram was a rather trivial statistical object, sort of a bar graph with the gaps removed to save space. I never realized that statisticians actually find histograms to be useful!

A modern data-centered approach to statistics starts with viewing the data in a variety of ways. What is meant by viewing the data? Features of interest to a statistician are the overall shape of the data, symmetry, the location and the spread, existence of outliers and evidence of clusters or gaps. A histogram with a scale on the horizontal axis is generally useful for showing all of these features.

One application of the humble histogram is determining if a set of data is approximately normally distributed, though a histogram is most effective with for this purpose if the dataset is large. Normality is a pre-condition for certain analyses of data. As we examine the limited data from the F exercise we can immediately see the groupings. We can see the four data points that fall in the first group (-0.5 to <19). Then we see a gap in data points in the next category, followed by 4 data points in the third category. While all these points are falling "normally" it would make me want to know why there is such a gap. A little research on this would have brought us to the conclusions we arrived at in the Lesson's of the F's chapter, that while normal, our procedure was open to many interpretations and therefore not conducive to productivity.

The Scatter Diagram

This tool starts to get into some of the more sophisticated analysis methods that an established QA system might want to use.

I have used it with organizations that want to compare two variables that affect each other. A typical diagram looks like this:

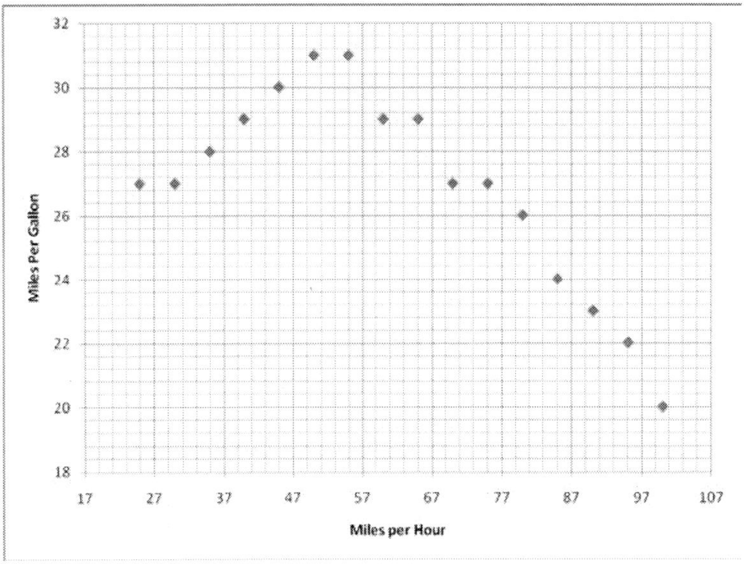

In this example we are comparing speed vs fuel consumption for an automobile. Now, I just made up these numbers, but they are within reason. The plotting of the data points was easily accomplished using standard graph paper and the data collected by a driver doing basic QC collection. From here it gets a little more difficult. There are calculations that we would make to determine the line of best fit. The software program we purchased on the internet for less that $200 does this, and many more, types of calculations for us.

Once we run this through our software it brings up a diagram like this:

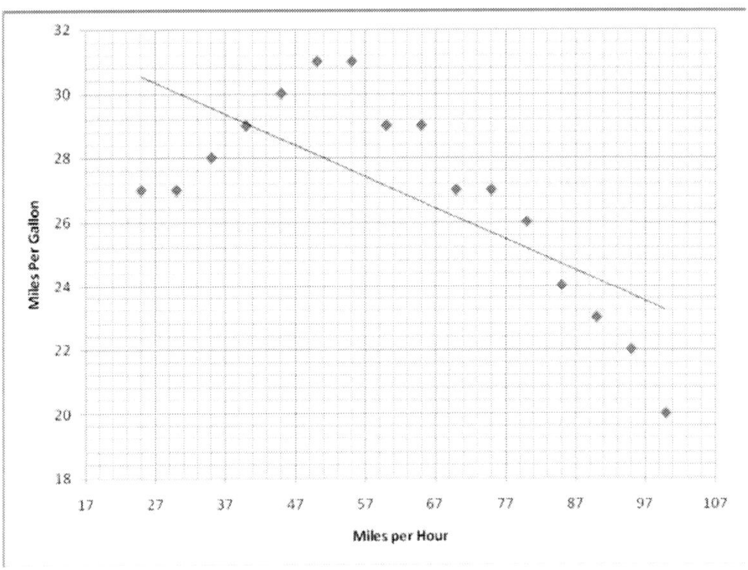

While this example is quite simple, the conclusion seems obvious, that we should drive this vehicle around 50 mph to save fuel. However as astute business people we also need to consider other issues, like increased delivery travel times and what they might cost us. So the line of best fit in this scatter diagram shows us the variation in our fuel consumption at different speeds and this will help us determine when it is advantageous to increase speed to decrease travel time or visa-versa.

We have just explored some of the basic ways to take a picture, make a visual representation of what we do. There are many other tools and diagrams that are equally as productive as the three we showed you. As your QA system evolves you will begin to search some of these out, since you now realize what they can do for you and your organization. Sometimes things that are obvious when presented visually are hidden by the everyday operations of our business. Our expertise in a particular field can be as detrimental to the success of our business as a lack of experience can be. Who ever coined the the phrase, losing sight of the forest, for the trees, was truly a visonary. And while, there are some very sophisticated tools to really disect and analyze our business and its procedures, don't let the fear that this is too complicated for your business stop you from looking into this aspect of analysis. Its rewards vs cost return will make you and your associates very happy. The improvement in output will make you more competative, because your product will be safer, better and more consistant than your competitions.

Chapter 7

My Quincunx and You?

"Statistical Process Control for Dummies"

Do you begin to sweat?

Do you get that "queasy" feeling in your stomach?

Most people do when they hear the word statistics. Unfortunately statistics and mathematics are important in the development and maintenance of a good quality assurance system. Statistical Process Control, or SPC, is the most widely used form of process control.

Does this mean that you have to go back to school to refresh your mathematical prowess? No. With just a general knowledge of the application of statistics a novice can navigate the statistical tools necessary to analyze a process or system performance.

Sol and I used to refer to ourselves as teachers. We now call ourselves facilitators. The primary reason for the change was to make our title fancier so we could charge more for a class! But more important, facilitators denote the idea of making a difficult topic easier to understand. It is the job of a teacher, now facilitator, to take a subject, such as statistics, and bring it to the level of understanding of the student. The facilitator should teach to the most basic level of the class. This is sometimes frustrating to the facilitator, but it defines the very purpose of the facilitator's mission. I have found that this skill is rare in most facilitators and teachers. I truly believe that good teachers or facilitators have an inborn gift for this talent.

The best way to teach a subject is to impart it, explain it, illustrate it, demonstrate it, and then review it! In order to teach statistics, as used in a Quality Assurance Program, I found that the students need a basic understanding of the foundation of statistics.

The foundation of statistics is based on a concept known as the "normal distribution curve" or bell shaped curve.

This reminds me of the true story of Quasimodo.

(Note from Sol: Dennis often digresses into his "true" stories. While there is usually some

underlying message, I can't help but get the feeling that I am in a Catskills resort comedy lounge sometimes. But, I will let him go on.)

Quasimodo was the famous bell ringer of Notre Dame. One day Quasimodo's brother showed up looking to be a bell ringer just like his brother. Unfortunately Quasimodo and his brother fought for the job of ringing the bell. One day the fight turned tragic when Quasimodo threw his brother from the bell tower. A crowd of people gathered around the body. One man in the crowd exclaimed, "What happened here, does anyone know this man?" another replied, "No, but he is dead ringer for his brother!"

The Quincunx

Since I must explain the normal distribution curve, I needed to find the best way to illustrate and demonstrate it. In my research, I discovered that this wheel had already been invented. The bean machine, also known as the quincunx (pronounced Quintox, don't ask me?) or Galton box, is a device invented by Sir Francis Galton to demonstrate the law of error and the normal distribution.

The machine consists of a vertical board with interleaved rows of pins. Balls are dropped from the top, and bounce left and right as they hit the pins. Eventually, they are collected into one-ball-wide bins at the bottom. The height of ball columns in the bins approximates a bell shape curve.

The Quincunx Machine

I own a quincunx machine, don't you?

There are many uses of the machine in teaching statistics. Sir Francis Galton invented the machine primarily to show that in a truly random system there is always a pattern made by the data.

The pattern is the bell shaped curve. So, if you have a bunch of data that form a bell shaped curve, you have a system that is considered normal.

In order to see the shape of this data we will have to order the data and count how many times each data point occurs. There is a tool used to do this very thing. The tool is called a Histogram. We talked of this tool earlier in the book and now we're going to expand a little on it.

In statistics, a histogram is a graphical display of tabulated frequencies, shown as bars. It shows what proportion of cases fall into each of several categories. A histogram differs from a bar chart in that it is the area of the bar that denotes the value, not the height, a crucial distinction when the categories are not of uniform width. The categories are usually specified as non-overlapping intervals of some variable. The categories (bars) must be adjacent.

The word histogram is derived from Greek: histos 'anything set upright' (as the masts of a ship, the bar of a loom, or the vertical bars of a histogram); gramma 'drawing, record, writing'.

A histogram can be constructed by segmenting the range of the data into equal sized bins (also called segments, groups or classes). For example, if your data ranges from 1.1 to 1.8, you could have equal bins of 0.1 consisting of 1 to 1.1, 1.2 to 1.3, 1.3 to 1.4, and so on.

The vertical axis of the histogram is labeled Frequency (the number of counts for each bin), and the horizontal axis of the histogram is labeled with the range of your response variable.

You then determine the number of data points that reside within each bin and construct the histogram. The bins size can be defined by the user, by some common rule, or by software methods

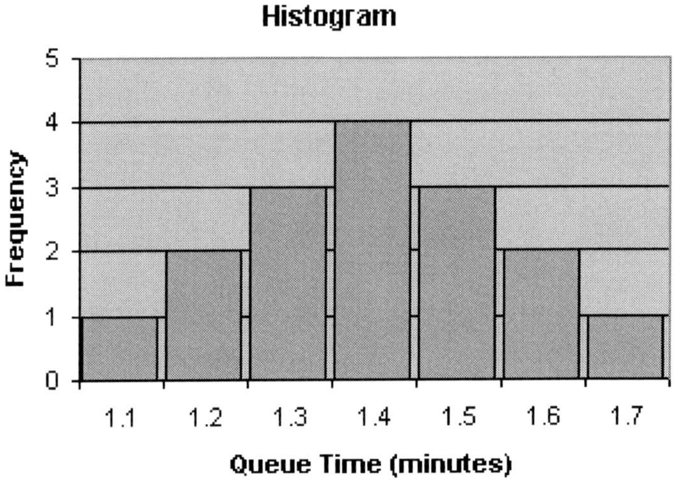

Chapter 8

Dumpster Diving

"What can I do with this non-conforming product?"

It is my hope that you will never have non-conforming material coming out of your processes. After all if you follow the advice already given, the probability of producing a bad product should be very low.

However, the production of non-conforming material is inevitable. In our seminars we teach that reducing the variation of your processes will lower the possibility of producing a bad product. It is important to remember that you must also center the normal distribution curve so that your central tendency is between your specification limits. A bell shaped curve that is shifted to the right or left can and will produce bad product.

Centering the normal distribution curve has been mystically called "Process Capability Studies" or Cp. Just remember that the mean or average of your data must be as close to the nominal specification as possible. There are plenty of computer programs that can perform this task. Some of them cost a little over $100 dollars. I would recommend getting one of these programs if you have a hard time with math.

Another concern with output of a process is this. Is the entire normal distribution curve within the specification limits? In other words, is the curve so “fat” that the tails fall outside of the specification limits? This type of analysis also had a mystical name. It has commonly be referred to a “Process Performance Studies” or Cpk. What I like about Cpk is that the formulas do give a quantifiable percentage of non-conforming material being produced. Again I would suggest getting a good computer program to help in these studies. Most computer programs that have process capability will have process performance build into them as well. Sol discovered an excellent program that simply attaches itself to Microsoft Excel. This program can easily build control charts, pareto analysis, and other SPC functions from Excel spreadsheets. The program also has the ability to perform process capability and process performance analysis.

OK, so what do we do with all this non-conforming material? The traditional Quality Assurance Program will channel all out non-conforming to the “Material Review Board” or MRB. What is a material review board other than another acronym for us to memorize.

You can think of the MRB as a court. The non-conforming material is marched into the court to face the judges. The judges usually consist of some engineers, some production personnel, and, of course, our quality assurance people. They look at each piece of non-conforming material and render a verdict. Now, keep in mind that the corrective action has already been initiated and preventive action has been put in place so that this horrible problem will never occur again. So we turn our attention to the “bad” product before us.

The judges will look at the product and render one of four possible sentences for this product.

The first disposition would be SCRAP IT! Throw into the dumpster it can’t be saved!

Most companies should try to avoid this option especially if the product was expensive to make. There must be something that we can salvage from this product? Which brings me to a alternate disposition.

"Find the gold coin in the field"

Yes it is the salvage disposition. This kind of disposition is already being done in the computer and PC board industries. Many of the components on PC boards and in computers are made of precious metals such as gold and silver. There are plenty of companies that will be happy to pay for this non-conforming material. Examine your scrap and see what is in it. Ask yourself some questions like, "Can I melt the material down to reproduce a good product or produce another type of product." This would be a type of recycling of the scrap material.

Another verdict of the judges could be to "REPAIR" the item. Now, a repaired item can not be sold as new. Although it has been tried by some companies. In most cases a repaired or refurbished item can work as well as the new product. Contact your customers and ask them if they would use a repaired item if the price was *reduced* of course! If not, I am sure there is customer out there that would love to take that product off your hands. Keep in mind that the repair verdict could be the most costly since you have to run the product through some type of refurbishing production and then sell it for less!

The third verdict is to “REWORK” the item. Wait a minute, isn’t repair and rework the same thing?

No, rework means that you can bring the product up to its original configuration so that it is new. It is possible to sell reworked product as new since it has not left the manufacturing cycle yet and can be brought up to full customer standards. Rework is not as costly as repair because for the most part you can sell the product as new. Keep in mind that a reworked product must look and work, just like a new product.

The fourth verdict that can be rendered by the MRB judges is a declaration! “USE-AS-IS.”

What does this mean?

Is the product bad or not? "Use-as-is" implies that the non-conformance does not affect form, fit or function of the item. The non-conformance may be cosmetic.

Warning, a use-as-is disposition can be a customer complaint in the making. If the customer notices the defect without disclosure by the company, the customer may see that as a quality deficiency and cause more reputational damage to the company than the money saved by the disposition.

Remember what is considered garbage by one is gold to another.

Dr. Edwards Deming demonstrated statistical control and management techniques in his seminars. He uses an elaborate experiment called the "Red Bead Experiment."

In this experiment volunteers from the audience are asked to produce white beads by scoping up a mixture of red and white beads with a scoop panel. The panel has dimples to hold the beads as they are scooped up. Each scoop does capture white and red beads. The object of the game is to produce white beads but, the result always has some red beads in it.

What do we do with the red beads. Dr. Deming says, “Find a customer for the red beads.” Just like we have people who will dumpster dive, we have people who will buy your non-conforming material.

Have you ever seen the production of the Pentium chip? The process of producing a Pentium chip always yields about 20 percent defective chips. These defective chips only function properly about half the time. Some function less than half the time. As a matter of fact the production yields of Pentium chips are rated. The chips that test 100% good get a rating of “A” and the others get ratings of “B” and below as they go down in quality. Well, intel has found a customer for the “A” chips. They go into computers and complex electronic devices. The “B” chip are sold to toy manufacturers to go into some of the new interactive devices and dolls . The toy company is not as concerned about the chip working 100% of the time. The “B” chip is lower in price and efficient enough for the toy to perform acceptably by its customers.

So, the next time you produce output that is not what your particular customer wants, find a customer that wants what you inadvertently produced.

Chapter 9

The Dead Parrot Speaks

"Corrective Action and Root Cause Analysis"

Once upon a time there was a man who walked into a pet store and asked the clerk, "I am a lonely person and I am looking for a pet that will talk to me. Do you have something that will do that?" The clerk answered, "Oh yes, we have this parrot that will talk all day to you." The man replied, "Great, I'll take it." With that the man happily left the shop with the parrot. A few days later he came back to the shop. He said, "I bought this parrot a few days ago and you said it would talk to me. It has not said a word since I got it. What's wrong?" The clerk answered. "Hmmm..I don't understand, maybe you need to buy some toys for it to play with. We have a little bell here and a ladder. The parrot will walk up and down the ladder and play with the bell. He will be happy and then he will talk." With that the man bought the bell and the ladder and went home to give them to his parrot. A few days later the man returns to the store. He said with disgust, "OK I bought the ladder and the bell and put them in the cage and now the parrot is dead!!" The clerk responded with surprise, "I don't understand the toys always work! Did the parrot say anything before he died?" "Yes" responded the man. "Right before he died he said, 'who moved the ladder'?" Here's the moral to the story. Corrective action does not always address the root cause of the problem and can even make the problem worse.

Ok, your procedures are all written. You made your check sheets and are ready to audit your processes. You begin to audit. What happens when you find a problem? Someone is not following the procedure. Maybe the procedure is bad. You discover a broken part. You have some customer complaints about the service they received. The process is producing non-conforming material?

All Problems Demand Corrective Action

I need to speak to the stigma that is associated with corrective action. Most people think of corrective action as a *disciplinary task*. Nothing could be further from the truth. Corrective action is an essential part of *process improvement* and should be viewed as such from everyone in the company. Since corrective action is an essential part of process improvement, it must address the following:

1. Cite the requirement violated – *verbatim*.

It is important to note that the corrective action report must be as clear as possible. It should state the requirement verbatim so that everyone who reads it knows without a shadow of a doubt what the law is.

2. Use simple plain terms.

Remember the corrective action must be understood by all who read it. The use of acronym and special terms must be avoided.

3. Set a time limit for response.

The corrective action must be answered by the department that *owns the process*. Unfortunately it is human nature to procrastinate. If you do not set a time limit, the corrective action will never be answered. The time limit for most companies is 30 days. Keep in mind that the problem must be fixed *immediately* and prevention plan is due in 30 days.

4. Response MUST address *ROOT CAUSE(s)*!

This is probably the hardest part of corrective action. Root cause analysis. We will address this very process shortly.

5. Re-audit to assure compliance

The answer to the corrective action must address a plan to prevent the reoccurrence of the problem. It is important for the QA department to audit that process again to assure that the improved procedures and plan was effective.

Root Cause Analysis

Analytical skills do not come naturally to most people. We need help in order to organize our thinking.

The Fishbone Diagram

In our seminars, Sol and I teach the Fishbone diagram. It is also called the *Cause and Effect diagram.* It was invented by Kaoru Ishikawa in the 1960s, who pioneered quality management processes in the Kawasaki shipyards. This tool helps organize the root cause analysis process.

Follow these steps to solve a problem with a Cause and Effect Diagram:

1. *Identify the problem:*
   Write down the exact problem you face in detail. Where appropriate identify who is involved, what the problem is,

and when and where it occurs. Write the problem in a box on the left hand side of a large sheet of paper. Draw a line across the paper horizontally from the box. This arrangement, looking like the head and spine of a fish, gives you space to develop ideas.

2. *Work out the major factors involved*: Next identify the factors that may contribute to the problem. Sol and I like to use the 6 inputs to any process identified by Dr. Deming. Draw lines off the spine for each factor, and label it. These may be *people* involved with the problem, *methods, equipment, materials, measurement, or environment*. Try to draw out as many possible factors as possible. If you are trying to solve the problem as part of a group, then this may be a good time for some *brainstorming*.

Sol and I don't use brainstorming much. We don't have the equipment necessary.

Using the 'Fish bone' analogy, the factors you find can be thought of as the bones of the fish.

3. *Identify possible causes:*
   For each of the factors you considered in stage 2 brainstorm possible causes of the problem that may be related to the factor. Show these as smaller lines coming off the 'bones' of the fish. Where a cause is large or complex, then it may be best to break it down into sub-causes. Show these as lines coming off each cause line.

4. *Analyze your diagram:*
   By this stage you should have a diagram showing all the possible causes of your problem that you can think of. Depending on the complexity and importance of the problem, you can now investigate the most likely causes further. This may involve setting up investigations, carrying out surveys, etc. These will be designed to test whether your assessments are correct.

Example:

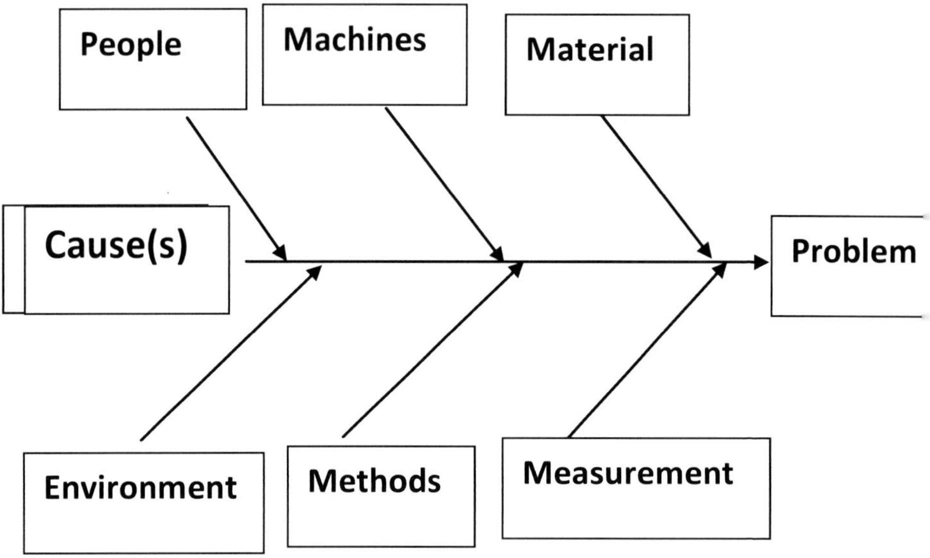
People
Machines
Material
Cause(s)
Problem
Environment
Methods
Measurement

Once the major spines are created, you then brainstorm possible causes in each category.

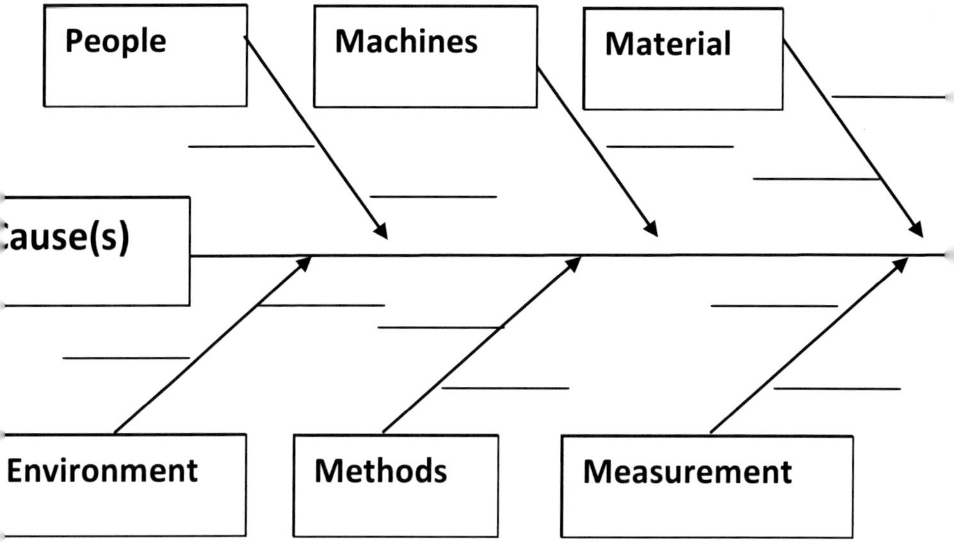

The major spines provide the focus of the brainstorming session. For example, the team will focus on Environment. They think of all environmental factors that might have contributed to the problem.

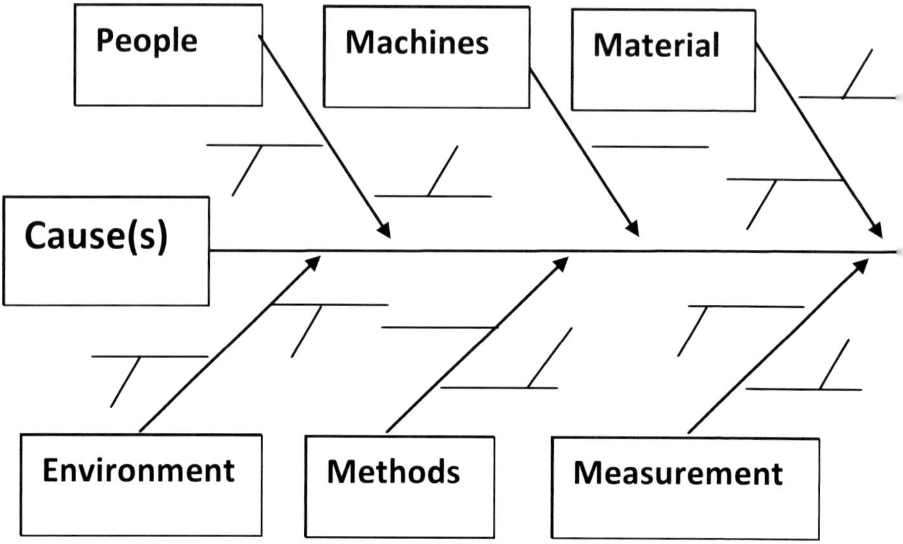

Yes even the subcategories can have causes as illustrated in the fishbone diagram above. Now let's take a look at a real example of root cause analysis using the fishbone diagram.

Sol and I were at the Toronto airport to catch an Air Canada flight to Vancouver. The flight was to leave at 6:30AM and it was a cold morning. We noticed that all the planes in our gate area were coming to the gates 45 minutes late. Our plane was also 45 minutes late. When it finally arrived, there was a mad dash to get everyone on board. They rushed to load the plane and the flight attendants were slamming the overhead bins closed and finally the plane pushed back from the gate. The plane stopped for a minute and then pulled back to the gate. The captain spoke through the PA system, "Sorry folks, we got a long flight ahead of us and we discovered that there is no water for the restrooms on the plane." How did that plane push back from the gate without any water on it?

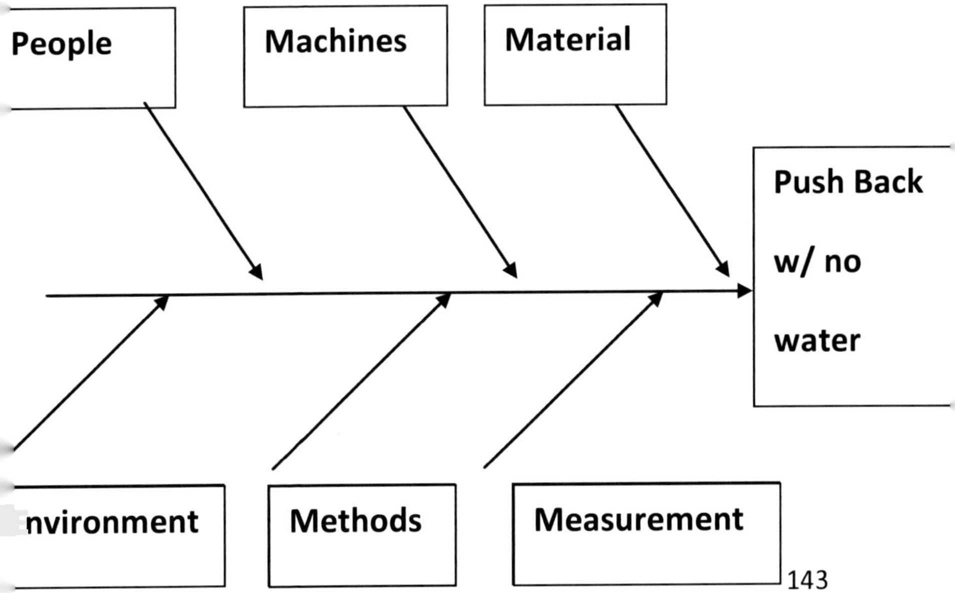

First select the major spine categories. Most teams use the 6 Deming inputs as illustrated here.

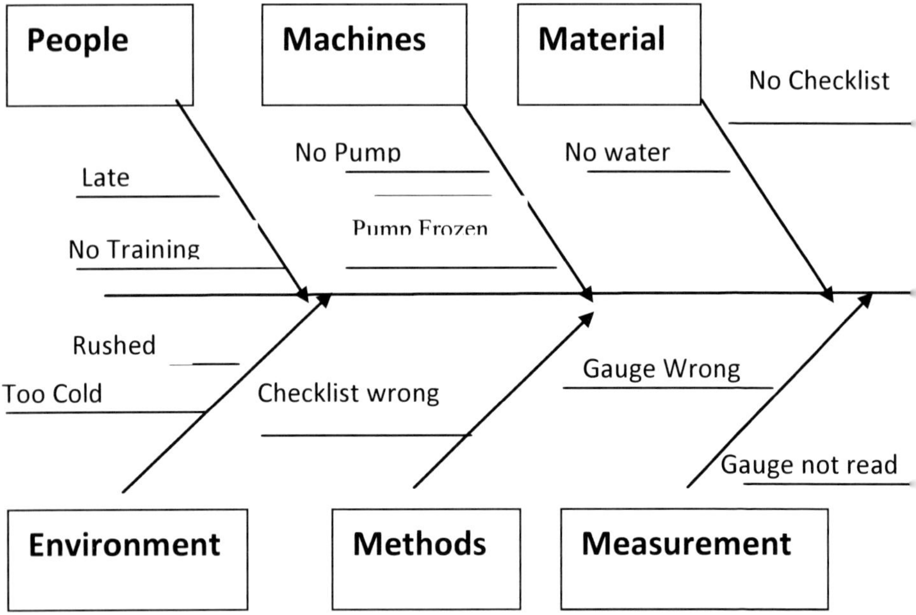

You can start to see that the fishbone is growing. The major spines help focus the groups' attention on a specific area. The group then begins to brainstorm causes within those spine categories.

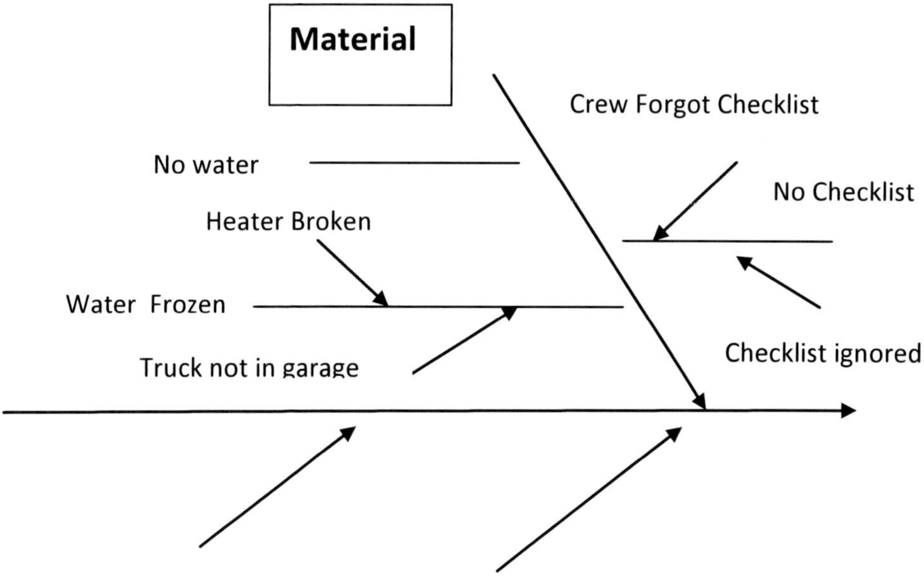

As illustrated here, each spine can be broken down to their causes. The process can continue even into each cause from the subgroup. I should note that the fishbone diagram does not need to be complete in one session. Sol and I have seen brainstorming using fishbone diagrams that lasted days. It is the tool that focuses your attention on a particular characteristic.

There are other tools that can be used to accomplish root cause analysis. Here are a few:

"The 5 Whys"

The five why's is a very simple tool to investigate the root cause(s) of a problem. The process begins with the problem. A group or team is formed. The team begins by asking the question, "Why did this problem occur?" The team will formulate several possible causes. These causes are written down. The team then focuses in on each cause and asks the same question. "Why did this cause occur?" The process continues with each of the sub causes identified. The process of asking why continues. By the time the team gets to the fifth why, you usually have a good picture of the "root causes" of the problem. The five whys is best used in conjunction with one of the other root cause analysis techniques.

Another excellent tool for root cause analysis is the "Fault tree" analysis. This is a pictorial technique that begins with the problem at the head of an organization chart. See the example below.

Here is an example of the fault tree analysis dealing with the lost baggage at an airport. Each level consists of possible areas of cause for the previous level. Once the diagram is completed, it easy to see the possible root causes of the original problem.

All of these tools mentioned provide a systematic way of focusing our analysis is specific areas. But, they also provide "*Objective Quality Evidence*" of the root cause analysis. These diagrams once finished should be a vital part of the Quality Assurance records of the company. There are other tools that can be used for root cause analysis but, go beyond the scope of this book. There is one unique areas I wish to explore in this section.

"Success Analysis"

Most managers of most companies have a traditional paradigm that needs to be addressed here. We as Quality Assurance specialist often focus our attention on the management of *failure*. In fact we called this section of the book *Failure Analysis*. We spend our time coming up with tools to analyze problems. We are so focused on problems that we fail to see and acknowledge our successes. I would like to introduce a concept I call “Success Analysis.” Why can’t we use the very tools mentioned here to help us analyze success! For example: Let’s say we provided our customer with outstanding service or produced an outstanding product. Take the time to ask your self, “How did we succeed here?” By analyzing success we can identify paths and procedures that work! Once we have identified our success patterns, we can then seek to improve upon them.

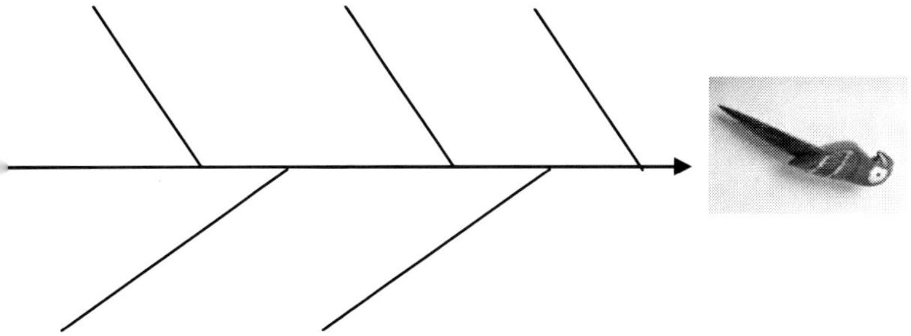

Chapter 10

Or

The End or the Beginning?

Well we have taken a bunch of the basic requirements that would make your QA system begin to function. We've tried to lay out the philosophies behind the requirements and a simple way to begin the processes. In our years in the business, both conducting seminars and working directly with companies and organizations, we have encountered all kinds of resistance to the implementation of a system. Many of these nay-sayers would have you believe the development of a Quality Assurance program is a tedious and complex task. Once again, we have found those who would say this usually have some sort of vested interest in helping establish your program.

I must admit that both Sol and I have made some people very upset with us. Our job is to take what appears to be difficult and bring it to the level of the person who needs to understand what is going on. Let's face it, most of us are NOT experts in Quality Assurance. You just want to stay in business and hopefully grow your business. This book has presented the basic tools needed to accomplish this. Once you understand what these components are and what they can do for you, the rest will be so much easier. There are many people in this world who have made a small fortune, hiding the basic facts and presenting this QA mentality as something mystical, filled with major technical and mathematical processes that can only be implemented by hiring their firm. You should now understand, that while as your company grows, the program will become more and more sophisticated, all these more advanced methods will still hold their foundation in the basic principles of this book.

In fact the book can be summed up in this simple statement:

"Meet the Requirements, Needs and Wants of Your Customer."

How do you know what your customers' want? Well that is a more difficult question, one which can make or break you. If you ever figure out how to determine exactly what your customer wants every time, give us a call and we'll invest in your company. But, until then we have a few suggestions.

So, you've decided that there is a need for your product or service. Are there others that have realized that need also? If not, your job is easy, for now. Believe me, someone will figure out about your niche and you won't be alone for long.

So how do you rise above your competition? By meeting the *WANTS* and NEEDS of your customer every time. Remember, YOU are the Frog! Don't be surprised by what your customers prefer.

“Know Your Customer!”

This is the key to your program. Knowing your customer needs and wants you can now establish the objective of your Quality system. As a quick aside, those of you who have organizations that have some sort of government or other regulatory restrictions must remember that these regulations are typically insisted upon by the government as a representation of the population, or better described, your customer. So, for all intents and purposes, that pesky government regulator is your customer, so get over it.

In our story the Frog thought she knew what whoever found her would want. What went wrong? She didn’t do her research, based upon her position in the forest what would be the probable demographic of the customer that would encounter her. Well, as it turns out it would have been a young boy.

Unlike the frog, you must know who your customer is and what their desires are.

Then you must establish the system that will provide that product or service *consistently*! The system should stop any abnormality from reaching your customer. The establishment of the Quality Assurance system will put in place the means to do this. Then following the system you have set up each and every day will, in short time, provide dramatic results.

In a Nutshell

Once you have established your goals you need to begin to form your written program.

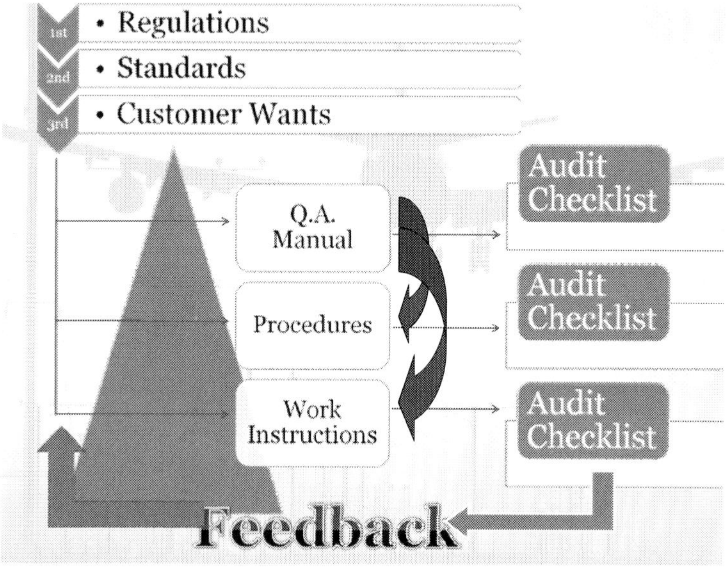

This is a graphic we use in our seminars. It shows the how the entire documented Quality Assurance program should be set up.

You start with the customer. Flow the customer requirements, needs and wants into your Quality Assurance Manual.

The QA manual then flows to all the documented procedures and work instructions throughout your organization. These procedures should be reviewed, and changed to improve them on a continual basis.

Once the procedures work to meet the process goals then, all the procedures and work instructions are made into audit checklists which will be used to assure the procedures and instructions are followed.

All the data that is collected throughout the system is analyzed on a continual basis to reduce the *variation* and make the process outputs more predictable.

The statistical analysis of the process now provides a basis for management to help improve the processes.

In a properly operating system, the Quality Assurance Program becomes a ***living*** program of continuous improvement.

As you have already seen in this book, *the implementation and maintenance of the Quality Assurance program is not as hard as you think!*

Both Sol and I have seen the vast benefits of an effective Quality Assurance System. It not only will make your company better and safer; it will also make it more profitable.

Yes, the story of the frog, is a simple story, but with a profound message. Life often comes at us at a fast and furious pace. It is at these times we need to get back to basics, to rely on the foundation we have built to carry the loads thrust upon us.

Postscript

Dennis and I try to live what we preach. We don't always succeed, but we know our failures would be bigger and more frequent if we did not prescribe to our own philosophies.

It is with this in mind that we offer our assistance with any questions you might have as you read this book, or hopefully begin to implement or improve your system. I am listing our email address below for you to contact us (within reason, please). We will try to help you out.

We do this, not just because we are nice guys, but because we believe that every good deed done reaps benefits, emotionally and more. So please feel free to drop us a line and we'll get back to you as soon as we can.

The DTI Training Consortium

www.dtitraining.com

www.dtiatlanta.com

webmail@dtiatlanta.com